FINDING MY MARBLES:

A STORY YOU CAN READ AND LIVE

Share your gifts

♡ , Clare

CLARE SENTE
TROY ADAMS

BOOK PUBLISHERS NETWORK

Book Publishers Network
P.O. Box 2256
Bothell • WA • 98041
PH • 425-483-3040
www.bookpublishersnetwork.com

10 9 8 7 6 5 4 3 2 1

Printed in the United States of America

    LCCN 2008941471
    ISBN10 1-935359-04-5
    ISBN13 978-1-935359-04-3

Editor: Julie Scandora
Cover Designer: Laura Zugsda
Typographer: Stephanie Martindale

*To my parents Olga and Ted Sente who gave me
everything I need to succeed.
To my sister Carol who is my best friend.
To Jen Pontrelli who helped add color and depth to
this story.
To my husband, Todd, and my children,
who are my everything.
To Troy who listened as I explained these
principles and then crafted a powerful story
around them.*

—CS

*To "Miss Griego" who gave me my first marble.
To my parents who have been an unfailing source of
support for as long as I can remember.
To my wife who stood by me during my own journey
out of the joyless zone.
To my children who are my daily joys.
To Clare who invited me to join her on this
creative journey.*

—TA

CONTENTS

FORWARD

Welcome. It is no accident that you are holding this book right now. Behind what may seem like a chaotic unfolding of your life, there really exists a higher order where everyone and everything are deeply connected and interdependent. There is a hidden harmony that connects all of us. For some, this harmony reveals itself only when reflecting back upon life experiences. For others, the harmony becomes apparent as it unfolds.

The beauty is that you were born to experience fully this hidden harmony and live out your true purpose, one that will bring you joy and help you benefit others. You were given an internal compass to lead you in the direction of your purpose. This compass is called your intuition or inner voice. Your inner voice doesn't critique you or flatter you like your ego. Instead, your inner voice guides you in a variety of ways using feelings, words, ideas, pictures, music, and encounters with others who have messages that will lead you in the right direction.

Feeling frustrated or quietly dissatisfied with your life is a common symptom indicating that you are heading in the wrong direction. If you are too busy to pay attention or distracted by external noise, you may miss quiet messages that would help you course correct. Purposefully slowing down and creating time for quiet reflection can help you be more sensitive to these messages. As you tune in to your inner voice and honor it, it will reveal even more to you.

Reflect back to a time in your life when you received advice from someone. How did you know what you were told was good? Think about how your body felt when you first heard the advice. Did the message create a negative reaction? Or did it resonate within you? When you receive good advice, something inside you recognizes that it is consistent with your own inner wisdom. And when this resonance happens within you, it feels good. It feels like home.

The second way you can know that advice is good is by applying it and observing the effects in your life and in those around you. This book presents powerful principles woven into a heart-warming story. But it isn't just a story to read. We invite you to check with your intuition as you are reading. Ask yourself, "Do these words move me to think about ways to improve my life?" We hope that by reading this story you will begin to see the world in a different way. It has been said that when you change, everything else around you changes.

We invite you to be open to the idea of listening, trusting, and acting on your intuition. Wherever you are in your life journey right now, we have one intention for you. It is our desire that the story you are about to read be one that helps you hear the invitation from your inner voice to move toward your true purpose.

Joyful reading,
Troy and Clare

CHAPTER 1

MARBLES

Marbles was the most peaceful little coffee shop in Chicago. Just outside the front door, the city buzzed with the dissonance of afternoon rush-hour traffic combined with the roaring and squeaking of the nearby El Train. On the sidewalk, pedestrians hurried as they shouted into their cell phones to be heard over the deafening noise.

The interior of Marbles seemed a world away from this bustle. Soft guitar music floated down from overhead speakers and blended with the aroma of freshly ground coffee beans and sweet pastries to create an atmosphere of sensory serenity.

The employees attended to their patrons in an effortless flow. Not even the occasional growl of the coffee grinder could break the harmony within Marbles. Customers quietly ordered from the menu which included warm cinnamon rolls made fresh daily, intriguing varieties of roasted coffee, hand-blended herbal teas, and the best cup of hot chocolate in Chicago.

A serene atmosphere *and* a tasty warm beverage is a recipe for satisfied customers. And the customers at Marbles were that and more. They were *peaceful*. They had *found* their marbles.

 The tranquil door tone announced a new arrival. A woman in her mid thirties cautiously peered into Marbles then tentatively entered. A few regulars looked up and smiled at the newcomer, but Edith did not return their looks or smiles. She could not recall when she had stopped looking into the eyes of strangers. But she was certain that, if anyone looked into her eyes, they would recognize the hurt and distrust, and she would be exposed. She felt too vulnerable to let that happen, so like most elevator riders, Edith focused her gaze upward and looked towards the menu. She edged forward with the intention of ordering, but the unfamiliar menu and surroundings proved a bit overwhelming, and she stopped several feet in front of the counter.

Edith needed more time before committing to a specific order, so she did what she usually did in an uncomfortable situation; she studied the interior layout of her surroundings. For as long as she could remember, Edith had been fascinated with interior design. When she was eight years old, her parents had allowed her to rearrange the living room. It had taken her the entire day to measure dimensions and draw several designs. Her parents, who rarely complimented her on anything, had both praised her creativity and even adopted one of her plans. She had discovered a gift for organizing interiors. How ironic that she had such disorder and chaos inside her life.

In Marbles, she noticed a unique combination of round and rectangular tables arranged neatly to the left and right sides of the counter. Small blue vases graced each table with a sprig of purple and yellow wildflowers. Above her, soft light cascaded from paper-shaded hanging lamps and radiated in overlapping circles on the counter, reflecting light off the metallic flecks in the marble counter top. The only thing that seemed out of place was the artwork. Edith scanned all of the walls. Gold-framed collages of images and words were displayed in vertical columns three-high on every wall. They were abstract and colorful, but their placement really disagreed with her design sensibilities.

A man and woman stepped in front of her to order, and Edith was relieved for the new distraction. The woman wore a chic bolero jacket over a yellow knee-length dress and black, stiletto heels. Silver jewelry on her wrists and neck accentuated her every movement. Her brown eyes sparkled as the woman quietly laughed with her partner. She looked so put-together and happy.

Edith looked down at her own wrinkled clothes and scuffed shoes. Without thinking, she touched the top of her hair hoping that her grey roots were not visible. Somehow, she just could not pull things together. It took too much energy; energy that she just did not have. She felt as if she had no control over anything in her life, not even her clothes or her hair. But it was worse than that. In her honest moments, she would admit to herself that she felt like an emotional hostage in a place where joy could not enter and pain could not leave.

It was Edith's turn to order, and she could delay no longer, so she stepped up to the counter. Her eyes were drawn to the glass bowl filled with brightly-colored marbles placed next to the cash register. *Marbles—how clever*, she thought. "Will you trust me to recommend the best hot chocolate you have ever tasted?" asked the kind voice from behind the counter. Edith looked up to find a woman with a welcoming face, patiently holding a purple ceramic mug. "May I ask your name?" Edith cleared her throat once and answered, "Edith." The server removed a stainless steel canister from a quietly whirring device that mixed and heated hot chocolate. In one smooth motion, she poured a dark chocolate ribbon into the purple mug and artistically added a swirl of whipped cream and chocolate shavings. Edith inhaled the delicious aroma. "That smells good, and it was so quick!" Edith said. The server smiled and replied, "I could tell that you needed hot chocolate so I started making it before you ordered. Here is your hot chocolate, Edith. May I get you anything else?" Edith was amazed but could not show it. She did not want to extend herself to this stranger, so she looked down and fumbled through her purse to pull out her money while shaking her head. "I'm fine," she said unconvincingly, "I'm fine." Her words dropped heavily to the floor. They were not true, and they both knew it, though neither of them said anything.

Edith received her change and mug of hot chocolate. As she moved toward the back corner of the store away from the windows, she glanced down to count her change then hesitated. "Is something wrong?" the same kind voice asked from behind her. Edith put her hot chocolate down on the nearest table and picked the shiny green marble out of her change. Holding it up, she turned and asked her question without saying a word. Motioning to a table along the wall, the gentle voice said, "Would you mind if I told you a story? I think you would enjoy hearing it."

CHAPTER 2

THE JOYLESS ZONE

E dith carefully placed her hot chocolate on the table and selected a chair against the wall. She sat and took a sip of hot chocolate. "Does it taste as good as it smells?" asked the server. Edith nodded and took another sip. The woman paused. She leaned closer and said quietly, "This story began about three years ago with a woman named Monica..."

 Monica was losing her marbles. She was sure of it. She could not shake the nagging feeling that a dark funk was following her everywhere she went. It felt sometimes as if her life was trapped in a dark, downward spiraling place that she referred to with great disaffection as the "joyless zone." One day, while sitting completely motionless in a traffic jam, she had decided to label her funk the "JZ." Saying just JZ took less energy.

Living in the JZ meant that nothing in her life was working and nothing, not one thing, *felt* right. She was stuck in the JZ and did not see any way out. Sometimes, in her rare quiet moments, she would try to identify when she had actually taken the first step into the JZ, but she never could. Monica was a mid-forty-something, single mother with two moody teenagers, an energy-sucking job that required her to travel too much, and a circle of friends who were either following her into the JZ or who had arrived there long before she had. Like Monica, none of them knew how they had fallen into the JZ, and none of them could tell her how to escape. She had gone to a counselor once who simply told her to re-examine and re-prioritize the things that were consuming her energy. The suggestion seemed plausible, so she purchased a red leather journal and started making a list of her energy suckers.

The exercise proved painful. After one week, she stopped because the writing had forced her to think about her life in a raw, emotionally naked way that was just too uncomfortable. She realized that her emotional bank account was overdrawn and there was no hope of deposits anytime soon.

First, there was her job. She invested energy in her work only so she could meet her financial obligations and support her children. She found no real joy in it, and she traveled more than she felt comfortable. The packing, the parking, the increasing scrutiny at the airport, and the frequently lost luggage were too much, even for someone who had a firm grip on her marbles.

For Monica, the extra travel annoyances seemed to compound her dark funk. When she went out of town for extended assignments, she would usually arrive in the evening, and all too often, her luggage would not arrive until the following afternoon. This routine had become so predictable that she began carrying a change of underclothes, a blouse, and some basic personal items in her purse.

When she was at the office, her work could best be described as colorless. Somehow, internal auditing was just not enough to light her creative fire. Her co-workers didn't help matters. There was Marty who insisted on forwarding every "hilarious email" then coming to her office five minutes later to see if she had read it yet. The response was always the same, "No, Marty, not yet." Sadly, he never seemed to notice the protective sigh that always accompanied her response, which was Monica's way of saying, "No narration, please." So Marty would explain the email in excruciating detail amidst snorts and guffaws that Monica had decided were a genetic flaw.

Then there was Cynthia who was so needy and fragile that after spending any amount of time with her, Monica was left exhausted. Once, Cynthia had spent a half hour in Monica's office talking about her fear of stairwells. "What if there is a fire and you get caught in a stairwell?" she had asked with panic in her eyes. That actually had given Monica an idea. She started taking the back stairwell up to the restroom on the next level so that Cynthia couldn't trap her.

The one co-worker that Monica appreciated was Tyrone, who just smiled and most important, did not drain her energy with irrelevant anecdotes or whiny complaints.

Her children, Josh, eighteen, and Marnie, fifteen, were good kids, but they always seemed a bit too happy when she left town and a little too annoyed when she returned. Lately, they just felt distant. She worried about them but did not really have enough energy to get past that teenage force field. For the most part, they all peacefully co-existed but rarely exchanged meaningful conversation. They could go for days without talking except for a cursory "Hello" or "Goodbye" or "Mom, I need some money." It hadn't always been like that, though.

Following Monica's divorce from their father eight years earlier, Monica, Josh, and Marnie had forged a tight bond with one another. As a team, they had endured the stresses of moving to a new town, starting in new schools, and making new friends. On most nights, laughter had reverberated off the walls of their small house as they had eaten dinner then played a card game or watched a movie together. They had created new traditions and new routines. Occasionally, one of them would be reminded of their former life, and sadness would interrupt the contentment. But Monica and her kids eventually had found in each other enough love and support to make their new life together grow and flourish. Now, she didn't even know who her children's friends were, what they enjoyed doing, or what they were feeling. What had happened?

Monica appreciated her friends, but they all seemed to have worse problems than she did. One by one, they all seemed to be spending more time in the JZ. Naomi complained that her marriage had deteriorated to the point that she and her husband rarely spoke. Susan had just lost her third job in fifteen months. Luis was drowning in credit card debt, and Evelyn's primary emotions were either anger or sadness.

The final push into the JZ for Monica had come when she had determined that she could not get a decent cup of hot chocolate anywhere in her neighborhood. Since her junior year in college, Monica had found comfort in a good cup of hot chocolate during many challenging times in her life. For just a few moments, she could lose herself in a deep, warm mug of creamy, perfectly frothed hot chocolate topped with a dollop of freshly whipped cream. A few sips from this delicious concoction always took her back to better times. The break and the memories helped her gather strength and left her feeling refreshed and rejuvenated.

There was that chain coffee shop on every corner, but they didn't seem to have an appreciation for good hot chocolate. The last time she had complained that her hot chocolate tasted like hot water and coffee grounds, the girl behind the counter had forced a glib smile and responded, "Three pumps of chocolate, miss, that is all we can add, just three pumps." Monica was losing her marbles; she was sure of it. She did not know where she had lost them, but she knew that finding them was the key to escaping the JZ.

 Edith took a sip of hot chocolate and gently set her purple mug back on the table. "That *is* the best cup of hot chocolate I have ever had. Thank you," she said. She thought for a moment then sighed and continued, "It sounds as if Monica and I live at the same address. And as near as I can tell, we have lots of neighbors in the joyless

zone. Sometimes it just feels as if it's impossible to escape." The words sounded hopeless. Edith fell silent. Her friend was content to be silent with her. Edith asked, "Did Monica ever find a way out of the JZ?"

Edith's new friend continued, "Monica felt as if the JZ was inescapable, too. But just when Monica was about to give up hope, something magical happened."

CHAPTER 3

FINDING A MARBLE

Grocery shopping was a necessary evil. On this trip to the local superstore, Monica's shopping list was small. "Cereal, orange juice, batteries, and toilet paper," she repeated to herself as she strode purposefully through the sliding front door. She grabbed a hand held shopping basket with her right hand without slowing down.

The basket would keep her from becoming distracted and would reinforce the small size of her shopping list. She was on a mission, and she was determined to avoid congestion and all shoppers on divergent trajectories. Her grocery shopping rules were simple: avoid protruding shopping carts and clogged aisles. Her goal was non-stop movement from the cereal to the orange juice to the toilet paper then finally to those AA batteries by the checkout counter. Just fifteen minutes and she would be on her way home. Monica looked at her watch, took a deep breath, and set off!

A traffic jam on the cereal aisle forced her to take a detour to the frozen food section. Orange juice was a no-brainer. She would buy two of the big cans then hope for family laziness so that the juice would never actually get mixed. *It will last longer that way*, she thought.

She snuck into the cereal aisle from the back of the store. *Three boxes of cereal should last a week*, she thought, *unless we eat cereal for dinner again.* She had decided that eating cereal for dinner was a very bad habit. It was true that cereal created fewer dirty dishes and was easy to put on the table, but her kids had discovered that cereal bowls were mobile. As soon as the milk was poured, they would abandon the dining room for more solitary confines. This always left Monica eating a bowl of processed, sugar-coated grain…alone in her dining room. *No more cereal for dinner*, she resolved while moving on to the paper-goods aisle.

Toilet paper required careful strategy. Monica preferred flowered patterns. Josh only liked white, and Marnie liked pink because it matched her bathroom. Josh would never use pink. This usually meant buying several packages, which really did not fit well in her shopping basket. Monica had tried explaining that, given the function of toilet paper, the color was insignificant. But the last time she had broached this delicate subject, there was drama, whining, and slamming doors. No, she wasn't going to die on that hill. The toilet-paper battle just wasn't worth the energy. White and pink toilet paper would have to do.

Batteries were always last because they were on the way out. *Why do they charge so much for these things,* she thought, *and how is it that an eight-pack can disappear in five days?*

Batteries in hand, she could smell victory. The challenge now was to choose the quickest lane so she could conclude her shopping mission.

She wondered if other people disliked grocery shopping as much as she did. She casually surveyed other shoppers. The signs were everywhere, the rolling eyes, the tapping feet, the glancing at watches. Nobody really wanted to be in the grocery store. Most of the time, the grocery store workers seemed oblivious to the fact that most shoppers just wanted to make their purchase and leave. They asked so many questions. "Do you want some stamps or ice? Paper or plastic? Did you find everything you need?" Monica considered herself a patient person, but there had been times in the grocery store when she wanted to scream, "Hurry up!" She was sure that she was not the only one who felt this way.

Monica resolved to get out of that store as soon as possible. Years of shopping-survival experience flashed through her mind: "Avoid the check-writers because they take too long, watch for slow walkers because slow walking means slow moving, and get in line behind mothers with small children." The last one seemed counterintuitive because kids can slow things down. But somehow, the motivation to get out of a grocery store can transform a mother with small children into an alien being with eight arms. Monica once emptied an overflowing grocery basket in record time while keeping Marnie from wiping her nose on Josh. She smiled as she remembered the chaos. *At least they were expressive then*, she recollected.

She began scanning the aisles for a mother with a small child. *This is an art form*, she thought, *even in the express lane.* She spied a man who had just completed his purchase, leaving only a little boy and his mother in line. They didn't appear to have anything to buy. *Perfect,* she thought. *That is my line.*

As she stepped in line behind the little boy, she overheard the mother explaining that the "nice cashier" needed the bag of marbles he was clutching so they could be scanned. "Conor, you need to give the nice lady the marbles so she knows how much they cost. Then she will give them back to you." Conor seemed hesitant. Giving the marbles to the cashier meant letting go, and that was hard to do. He reluctantly released his grip on the little bag of marbles, trusting his mother's word.

Conor looked about five years old. His baggy blue jeans were still a bit too long, but he would grow in to them. He had blue shoes that lit up every time he shifted his weight. *His feet must look like holiday lights most of the time,* Monica silently mused. His tussled red hair fell over his ears in a floppy, curly mess, and it looked like he might have to grow in to his ears as well.

Monica was anxious to leave the store, but something about Conor reminded her of happier times when she had taken Josh shopping as a little boy. Monica carefully observed Conor and his flashing shoes. His bright, sky blue eyes were accented by a string of freckles sprinkled from one cheek to the other. Judging by the residue around the corners of his mouth and on his red sweatshirt, he had very recently consumed a cinnamon roll. His boyish grin was genuine. He looked sublimely happy to be purchasing a small bag of marbles. She noted how he watched the cashier scanning his bag of marbles with breathless anticipation.

"That will be three dollars and twenty-three cents," said the cashier with a hint of kindness in her eyes. Conor produced a wadded up five-dollar bill from his pocket and thrust it toward the cashier without taking his gaze from the bag of marbles. Monica guessed that the money was a birthday gift from a relative.

The cashier efficiently made change and leaned over to give it to Conor. He had already opened the bag of marbles and was carefully admiring a green cat's-eye. His mother nudged him and motioned to the cashier, whispering something in his ear. He carefully placed the marble back in its bag and held out his hand to receive his change. He looked in utter amazement at the money in his hand. Judging by the expression on his face, Monica guessed that his brain was spinning a million miles a second, *I got a bag of marbles and money back too!* He stood glued to the spot, looking back and forth from his marbles to the money. He finally stuffed the money into his pocket and reached for the green cat's-eye again.

Conor's mother nudged him again and prompted, "Conor, what do you say?" Conor beamed brightly as if he had just remembered a secret. He looked directly at the cashier and said with childish sincerity, "Thank for my marbles." The cashier smiled at his joyous display of pure gratitude and replied, "My pleasure."

Then the magic happened. Conor removed the green cat's-eye marble and held it up to the light. "This is a good one," he said to no one in particular. Then, he resolutely extended the marble to the cashier and said, "Here, you can have this one." An awkward silence followed. The cashier looked at Conor then at his mother then back at Conor. "Thank you so much," she said, placing her hand over her heart. "That is the nicest thing anyone has done for me this whole week." Monica felt a lump rise in her throat, and her eyes began to tear up. She wondered, why did this simple gesture pull so hard on her heart-strings? The answer was suddenly obvious. She had just witnessed a demonstration of genuine gratitude, and it was a beautiful thing.

As Conor and his mother left the store, Monica unconsciously stepped forward. The cashier, now wearing a warm smile, predictably asked Monica, "Did you find everything you need?" Without thinking, Monica replied, "No, I didn't." Ignoring the cashier's confused expression, Monica asked, "Where can I find a bag of marbles?"

 It had been a few weeks since Monica had learned about gratitude from a five-year-old. While some things had *not* changed since then—both cans of orange juice were still in the freezer—some things had *really* changed. Monica felt as if she had started to find her marbles, literally. She had learned from Conor that gratitude is a beautiful thing to observe, but over the past several days, she had learned how wonderful it *felt*. That day in the store, it had taken her ten minutes to find her own bag of marbles. She did not really know why she was compelled to buy them. But she had added marbles to her purchases that day, and like Conor, she had selected a beautiful green cat's-eye that she had kept with her everyday since.

She held it in her hand several times a day, at first to remember the lesson of genuine gratitude she had witnessed. Gradually, however, she noticed that as she held her marble, she actually *felt* grateful. She found it easier to think of things that had occurred that day for which she was deeply grateful. It was as if the marble was somehow transforming her view of the world.

On a particularly bad day, she held the marble in her hand, and while nothing had happened that day for which she was at all grateful, she felt impressed to be grateful for opposable thumbs. That evening, she related her experience to Marnie, who predictably snorted, "Mom, that is SO lame!" But Monica insisted that having opposable thumbs was a really good thing. She challenged Marnie to mix up a pitcher of orange juice without using her thumbs. Marnie accepted the challenge, thinking it would be easy. Within minutes, they were both doubled over in deep, belly laughter, the kind that neither of them had felt at home for some time. It felt really good.

When Josh came home and found them in stitches, Marnie managed to explain to him between snorts why they were laughing. Josh rolled his eyes and muttered, "You two are crazy." Still laughing, Marnie handed Josh the orange juice and the pitcher and said, "Go ahead." He hesitated for a moment but accepted the challenge. He, too, failed miserably. And even though he was visibly irritated, he could not resist the force of humor, and soon, the three of them were wrapped in uncontrollable laughter. After all of them had given up, Josh put the orange juice, the pitcher, and the mixing spoon back in the freezer, and they all laughed again.

When the laughter subsided and her kids retreated to their rooms, Monica felt a deep sense of contentment. Both her children had looked at her with eyes she had not seen in some time. Eyes that said, "We are not sure what just happened, but we liked it." She saw this as an encouraging sign of progress. Something was happening to her. Something was changing her. She believed that her marble was helping her remember and create more gratitude.

Even at work she noticed a difference. She felt a bit more patient when her co-workers did something that had previously been bothersome. She could even tolerate Marty's email narratives. Once, she even read one of his emails *before* he came into her office. When he barged in, Monica complimented him on the very funny email. At first he looked confused because Monica had never before read one of his forwarded emails. He left still confused, but looked affirmed. Monica felt as if she had done a good thing for Marty even though she could not possibly keep up with all of his emails!

Her friends also noticed a difference in Monica. At first they thought her hair was different or that she had started working out. Naomi had come closest when she had commented one day at lunch, "Something just looks different in your face" then quickly guessed, "You have met someone!" Slightly amused, Monica teased, "Yes, I have met someone!" Thinking of Conor with his messy red hair and flashing shoes, she added, "And he is really cute!" She winked and smiled playfully at Naomi but left her hanging in suspense.

A few weeks of feeling grateful was starting to feel good to Monica. It was almost as if gratitude had taken her to a higher place from which she could see more possibilities. She was aware that she did not feel trapped in the JZ as often, but she also felt that her liberation was not complete. The bag of marbles was only the first step on the journey. Monica decided to continue noticing the things for which she was grateful but also to open herself up to other messages and other chance observations like the one she had so fortunately made that day in the grocery store. How grateful she was for the pure gratitude of that little boy Conor.

 Edith eyes were misty. She picked up the marble that had been sitting in front of her on a napkin. She held it up and asked, "Is this supposed to be a gratitude marble?" Her question was met with an affirmative nod. Edith set the marble down and stared at the table for a few silent moments. Looking up, she asked, "So am I supposed to carry this marble and remember to be grateful?" Realizing that the answer to her question was obvious, she continued, "What if there is nothing for which to be grateful?" Edith immediately looked down, suddenly feeling very vulnerable. She silently berated herself. She didn't even know this woman. How could she trust her? She felt a reassuring hand touch her forearm, "Opposable thumbs, Edith. If there is nothing else, be grateful for opposable thumbs." Edith nodded resolutely and placed the marble in her cupped hand. Her eyes, still moist from the power of the story, were filled with a new sense of determination. Edith looked up as if to say, "Please continue."

Edith had wandered into Marbles for a warm beverage. What she was served was a much needed and long overdue helping of courage.

CHAPTER 4

DAILY JOY

Monica was grateful for the train because she could get into Chicago quickly without the stress of driving a car. When she rode the train, she never had to worry about finding a parking place or getting stuck in traffic or avoiding bad drivers. The train was a very good thing she had decided. When Monica caught herself thinking grateful thoughts about something as mundane as the commuter train, she was pleased. She felt grateful, and she loved that feeling!

Just a few weeks earlier, the train ride would have been just another drain on her energy that sent her further into the JZ. A crowded train with standing room only was simply miserable. Even minor things, such as loud cell phone talkers, double seat takers, or an unlatched bathroom door slamming open and shut, would be very annoying. But today, despite waiting outside in the nippy April wind, Monica was grateful for the train.

Monica felt in her coat pocket for her favorite marble—a green cat's-eye. She held it in the center of her hand, letting it roll from one side of her palm to the other. She looked about self-consciously to see if anyone was watching her. Nobody was. She pinched the marble between her thumb and forefinger and held it up to catch the sun's rays. This small glass orb had given her courage to take her first steps out of the JZ. "Conor," she whispered to herself and smiled.

As the train lurched forward to take her to work, her mind somehow connected gratitude and work. She laughed to herself. Could she ever be grateful for her work situation? She shook her head and decided that three weeks was not long enough to have evolved *that* far. No, work was still difficult to manage.

Things seemed better at home, though. Marnie had started saying, "Hi, Mom," and the three of them had actually eaten several dinners together in the past few weeks. Things were not perfect, but the atmosphere just felt better at home.

The train began to slow as it approached the next station. People bunched up around the doors to get off. Monica had always been amused by the way people pushed forward to get off the train while the people on the outside tried to get on. The trained jerked to a stop. Predictably, there was a muddle of bodies when people with opposing agendas collided between the open doors.

When the last few stragglers were entering the train, Monica's attention was drawn to a petite, older woman who glided onto the train after everyone else. She carried herself confidently, with her shoulders back and purpose in her steps. Her hazel eyes were framed by grey hair pulled back neatly in a bun. She wore a knee-length, pink skirt that was accented by a matching three-quarter-length jacket and a white silk blouse. Monica noticed that the buttons on her jacket were made out of ivory. The style of the suit reminded Monica of something that Jackie Kennedy would have worn, but the suit was impeccably maintained. *Very classy*, Monica thought to herself.

This woman carried herself with a quiet self-assurance. As she walked down the aisle, Monica noticed with mild alarm that she was violating an unwritten rule of the train. She was looking at people and smiling! Most people did not see her because they were texting, glancing absent-mindedly out the window, or reading. Monica could not help but watch her, and before she could look away, they had made eye contact. The woman did not look away either. Instead, she gave Monica the kind of warm and genuine smile usually reserved for relatives and good friends. Monica returned her smile half-heartedly then, out of habit, averted her gaze out the window. "Is this seat taken?" the woman said, motioning to the seat next to Monica. Monica slid over to the window seat and gave the woman her seat on the aisle. The doors closed, and the train began to edge forward. Monica could still feel the woman's eyes looking at her. She could not resist; she had to turn and look. The woman met her glance, smiled, and said, "Good morning." Monica hesitated, but something compelled her to engage with this woman. Monica turned slightly in her seat toward the woman and said, "Hello."

"Cecilia Hudgins," she said, extending her hand, "but my friends call me CiCi." "Monica Montoya. Nice to meet you." Monica paused, then added, "I really love your suit." CiCi chuckled a warm throaty laugh, "Thank you, my dear, but I believe it is what you might call vintage." Monica smiled feeling better about opening herself up. CiCi offered, "I bought it years ago but never wore it 'til last year. I was always saving it for a special occasion. Can you believe that? Saving it for a special occasion," she said, shaking her head and chuckling to herself.

CiCi continued as if she and Monica were close friends, "Well, I decided one day last year that it was time to use all the things I had been saving. Now, I wear my best clothes whenever I can, and I eat supper every night off my best china." She continued in a whisper as if she were telling a secret. "I even use the sheets that I always saved for my house guests," she said, nodding for emphasis.

Monica decided that she liked CiCi very much. Monica was gathering the nerve to ask what had prompted this major shift, but she didn't have to ask. CiCi continued voluntarily, this time with a hint of sadness in her eyes. "My Rupert died last year," she said, pausing to look out the window of the moving train. She added, "I was heartbroken and I guess a little ungrateful for a time." She turned in her seat better to face Monica and patted Monica's hand once as if to punctuate her next point. "Then it occurred to me that I had been blessed with so many good years with Rupert. And I had an abundance of wonderful things for which I had never really expressed proper appreciation.

"As I began to notice those things and to express gratitude, I gradually gave myself permission to use the things that I had been saving. I realized that I couldn't really be grateful for something if I didn't use it." Waving her index finger in the air, she said, "And, you know, an interesting thing happened. As I starting paying attention to feelings of gratitude, I started noticing even more things for which I was grateful." CiCi paused to look at Monica. She drew a deep breath and asked, "What are you grateful for Monica?"

Monica could tell that CiCi was studying her face and felt that she should say something, but the words would not come. She felt flushed and tingly at the same time. She could not believe that CiCi had just asked her about gratitude. What an amazing coincidence. CiCi touched her hand and asked in a sincere tone, "Are you all right, my dear?" Monica mustered a half-hearted smile and nodded, but CiCi smiled knowingly. They rode in silence for several minutes.

The train continued its rhythm, speeding ahead then stopping to exchange passengers. The seats around them were mostly vacant, which was unusual for a weekday commute. Monica glanced at CiCi and cleared her throat. She held up her marble. Showing it to CiCi, she said, "This is my gratitude marble. I carry it with me to remind me to find things—good things—that make me feel grateful."

Monica related the whole story from her feelings about the joyless zone to Conor and his flashing shoes to the present moment. Smiling and nodding at all the right moments, CiCi listened with sincere attention. She seemed to hang on every word and pick up every emotion. Even though Monica felt as if the words were spilling out in a flood, she sensed that CiCi was genuinely listening to her.

Monica finished breathlessly, "After three weeks, I feel so much better, but I am not sure what to do next." Monica stopped, not knowing what else to say.

CiCi put her hand on Monica's forearm and leaned closer. She whispered, "I think maybe I have a message for you." "You do?" Monica said, dabbing moisture from the corner of her eyes. CiCi's eyes twinkled. She continued, "About a week after Rupert died, I found a note he had written to me. It was a simple note telling me how much he loved me. I don't know when he was planning to give it to me. It didn't matter. It filled me up with so much appreciation that I cried the rest of that day. I cried plenty in the days after he died but those tears were tears of grief. The tears I cried after reading that note were tears of gratitude, and they felt wonderful.

From that day on, I tried to notice things for which I was grateful everyday. If I couldn't find anything, I would just read Rupert's note again. After a few weeks, I felt as if I needed to do something else, too. It was like knowing that I needed to grow but not knowing exactly what to do."

"Yes, that's *exactly* how I feel!" Monica exclaimed.

CiCi nodded then continued, "One day, I was cleaning out my closet, and I found this suit all covered in white plastic. I couldn't even remember what was inside the plastic. When I opened it up and saw the suit, I remembered how I had felt when I had bought it and how beautiful I had felt when I had tried it on. But I could not ever remember a time when I had worn it. I felt guilty for wasting money, not because I bought it, but because I never allowed myself to enjoy it. That is when I discovered the secret of finding daily joy—of wearing this suit, using my fine china, and sleeping on my best sheets. So that is the secret I have for you, Monica—sleep on your best sheets every night, my dear." CiCi smiled mischievously. "You need to find your own daily joy."

"Daily joy?" asked Monica.

CiCi leaned closer to Monica and squeezed her hand. "I must get off the train soon, so please listen." She continued, "I grew up in a time when service was a more noble virtue than it is today. Now, I believe that service is important; don't get me wrong. But if the practice of service means one's needs are permanently suppressed, that is a problem. The warning signs are saving new things just to keep them new and practicing denial out of habit until, eventually, the art of finding daily joy is lost."

"But how do you find daily joy?" asked Monica. CiCi chuckled. "The secret to daily joy is different for every person, but I can tell you something that might help. For years, I had a beautiful garden in our front yard. People would stop and admire it, and I would get comments in the grocery store and at church about my gorgeous flowers. Do you know why I started growing them? I always loved the smell of fresh flowers," she said, answering her own question.

CiCi suddenly looked solemn. She looked directly into Monica's eyes. "I loved the way they smelled, but I never cut any fresh flowers for my own home. I shared plenty of flowers with others, but I never allowed myself to experience that small daily joy. It makes me sad to think of all the small, joyful moments I missed."

CiCi started to gather up her things. Monica felt a sense of panic. She had so many questions. "This is my stop," CiCi said, "but I have something for you." CiCi reached into her purse and retrieved a small yellow daffodil pin. "Daffodils were always my favorite. Take this pin, my dear, and remember to find your own daily joy." The train slowed to a gradual stop. CiCi smiled at Monica and patted her on the cheek. "Daily joy," she said. Cecilia Hudgins stood and glided off the train just as elegantly as she had entered.

What would bring her daily joy? Monica knew that she needed to think of ways to find daily joy that were simple and inexpensive. The rest of the ride to work, she could think of nothing else. As she exited the train and began her walk to work, she felt buoyant. She wanted to raise her voice and shout with joy for she knew that she had just made another breakthrough. Already she had thought of three wonderful, beautiful, joyful things that she could begin doing that very day. Upon arriving at work, Monica sat at her desk and wrote down her three secrets to daily joy.

 Edith became aware of a dull buzz coming from other conversations in the coffee shop. She realized that she had been holding her breath, waiting for those secrets to daily joy. She blurted impulsively, "What were the secrets?" Edith looked longingly across the table, waiting. She *needed* to hear those secrets to daily joy! But with a look, she knew—the secrets were Monica's. Edith understood. She would have to find her own. Seeking affirmation, Edith said aloud, "There is no secret recipe to daily joy, is there? I mean, even CiCi said that the secret to daily joy is different for every person—right?" The warm smile and gentle nod from across the table told Edith that she was correct. Edith sat back in her chair and held her mug between both hands. She thought for a moment then said quietly, "I am in charge of my own daily joy?" She paused a few moments then repeated, this

time more firmly, "I am in charge of my own daily joy." Her eyes brightened, and she said up straighter as if the words had given her strength. One final time she declared, "I am in charge of my own daily joy!"

CHAPTER 5

TURN DOWN THE NOISE

Monica's first daily joy was walking away from work at lunchtime. Walking was the easiest of her "daily joys" to apply because she liked to walk and she still did not like work. Work sapped her joy, but walking replenished it. So everyday at noon, Monica simply walked away from work.

On most days, she would walk out the front door, take a deep breath, and pick a direction. It didn't matter where she walked, so she would walk until she felt compelled to turn left or right or to stop and rest. Walking cleared her head and invigorated her mind and body. Sometimes while she was walking, she felt as if everything in the world just worked perfectly. That usually lasted until she went back to work.

In a matter of days, walking started to open up her world. She saw new places and discovered new things. One of her first finds was a store three blocks from work that sold products, such as relaxing music, incense, scented oils, candles, and an excellent selection of books to soothe the soul. She could not resist purchasing a CD with a collection of classical guitar music called "Grateful Joy." She listened to the CD every evening because it created the mood she wanted to feel in her home. The music was quiet and contemplative, but it also had an energy that seemed to lift her up and keep her going. It reminded her of music she had once heard in Europe with her friend Joyce.

She had also found a place to get a semi-decent cup of hot chocolate. It was better than the hot chocolate served by the big coffee chain, but it still did not have that special something she was looking for.

Perhaps her favorite discovery was the park. It was a delightful spot amid the buildings with velvety soft grass, billowing oak trees, and a winding path. Beneath some of the large trees were quaint, wooden park benches painted in several pastel colors. She went to the place often and enjoyed the unusually mild May weather in Chicago.

The park became an unexpected daily joy. She decided that it held a renewing power for her. So Monica returned to the park on a regular basis, often sitting on one of the colorful benches to eat her lunch. Within a few weeks, she observed that other people had also discovered the renewing power of the park. She privately called them "park people." The park people included a few other working professionals, some high school students, and a pair of older African-American gentlemen.

One of these gentlemen in particular stood out. He had been on the same bench nearly every time Monica had gone to the park. Each time she saw him, he seemed genuinely happy. He had an engaging, radiant smile and sparkling eyes.

He always wore a grey fedora tilted slightly forward and to the left, but only when he was walking. The color of his hat nearly matched his hair. When he walked, he used a dark brown wooden cane with a bone handle to support himself. Monica noticed that he had a slight limp, but it did not seem to slow him down. When he sat on the bench, he removed his hat and placed it carefully on the seat next to him. He usually crossed his legs and planted one end of his cane to support his body. Monica noticed that he greeted everyone who passed by and visited with anyone who would stop long enough to tune in.

On a beautiful Tuesday morning in mid-May, Monica decided to escape work for an early lunch. She felt her heart leap as she left her building and turned toward the park. The thought of walking to her favorite daily joy was enough to make her happy, but today, she felt especially light. As she walked, she found herself holding her head up and smiling at complete strangers. She thought to herself, "I am acting like CiCi!" She laughed quietly at the thought.

As she approached the park, she could see Mr. Grey Fedora engaged in an animated conversation with his friend. Both of them were motioning wildly with their hands and speaking at the same time. Monica laughed. She called that type of conversation a collective monologue. She had watched collective monologues many times in staff meetings—everyone talking but no one listening.

She wondered what Mr Grey Fedora and his friend were talking about. What had them so excited? Curiosity got the best of her so she angled her course for a bench about fifteen feet behind them. Monica was going to eavesdrop! She rationalized that she needed to hear a conversation with some emotion. *I really need a job that includes good conversation,* she thought.

Mr. Grey Fedora had noticed her. As Monica passed behind his bench, he turned and smiled. Monica returned his smile. He seemed genuinely pleased and nodded in her direction, tipping an imaginary hat. His friend was not pleased at all. He had just made a brilliant point in their debate that had been missed. Monica easily overheard the chastisement, "Earl, I can't talk to you 'bout nothin' with these skirts around. You ain't payin' attention so I'm goin' home." He stood to leave but Earl gripped his arm. Still smiling, Earl said with amusement in his voice, "Sit down Ellis. You got no better place to go. No use squabbling over who makes the best cinnamon roll anyway."

Monica nearly laughed out loud. They were discussing the merits of a good cinnamon roll with the animation and enthusiasm of a presidential debate! Monica liked Earl's perspective and she liked his voice. It had a deep, gravelly quality that she found soothing. She thought he would be an interesting person to talk to about anything. She decided to ask Earl his opinion on cinnamon rolls the next time she came to the park.

As Monica ate her lunch, she looked around to see whether any other park people were there. Besides Earl, there was a young woman in her twenties who she had seen several other times. She usually dressed borderline professional with unique accents that clearly said she was following the dress code but she didn't like it. One day a few weeks back, she had worn a black pair of very baggy pants, a turquoise, long-sleeve t-shirt, a bright pink and tan plaid vest, and pointy red shoes. Monica remembered the outfit because she had never seen so many different colors worn together on one person. Last week, the young woman had her hair in multiple braids with purple and orange beads. She usually sat cross-legged on a bench while she ate.

Today, there was also a small gaggle of prep-school girls wandering diagonally across the park. One was jabbering away on a cell phone while another's thumbs busily tapped out a flurry of text messages. Two others appeared deeply engrossed in conversation, both of them loudly relating the details of their daily dramas. If they were like her daughter, Marnie, the conversation was probably centered around boys or annoying parents. However, it did not appear that either one was really listening to the other. Monica laughed to herself at the irony.

Monica was jolted out of her people-watching by a loud, headache-inducing sound. She looked around to find the offender, a large white truck turning left onto the street that ran adjacent to the park. The distorted music boomed into the open area and momentarily stopped all movement and conversation. But it wasn't the music that was paralyzing. The thumping bass was simply too much for the speakers to handle, so the music was accompanied by a heavy buzzing over-tone that felt like finger nails on a chalkboard. But neither the occupants of the truck nor the prep-school girls seemed to care about the buzzing.

The girls whooped and waved, and the driver added a honking horn to the chaos when he noticed the girls. So much noise caused by one truck. Monica wondered if she had been that noisy as a teenager. She couldn't have been. Not even Marnie and Josh were that noisy on a bad day. Soon the truck passed, and the natural ambient noise of the park was restored. Eating, walking, and talking resumed. Earl's friend was the first of the pair to say something. "What in the *purple monkey* was that?"

She could hear Earl clear his throat. "I'll tell you what that was, Ellis." Monica was immediately soothed by that deep, raspy voice. She turned her head to listen. "It was some kids who are confused about who they are and what they want outta life so they are trying to cover their confusion with noise. That noise keeps them numb to what is real but makes them feel connected to somethin' even if it's just empty noise. It's like those donuts you eat, Ellis. They make you feel good for a little while, but there is really nothin' in a donut that fills you up. It's all empty. It's all nothing. Those kids are living on emotional donuts, and they'll keep livin' that way until they learn to turn down the noise and tune in the peace."

Monica froze. Turn down the noise and tune in the peace. She felt the words ripple through her body. That was an unmistakeable message! She knew because she had experienced the same feeling when she had talked to CiCi on the train and when she had recognized the message from Conor. Turn down the noise…turn down the noise. That was it!

She heard nothing else that Earl said. Her mind began to focus on things in her life that were just noise. The television was always turned on. A radio was usually playing. Sometimes both were on at the same time. Why? Was she trying to cover up confusion? What was she trying to numb? She had so much to process.

Turn down the noise. How could she turn down the noise? How could she keep from consuming her own empty, emotional donuts? She rose abruptly to leave. She needed to walk. She needed time to brainstorm ways to turn down the noise.

 Edith was silent for a minute. "My television is noisy and annoying. I have no clue why it is always on. I think it covers up the fact that I live alone." Her voice trailed off. She looked at her watch and said apologetically, "I have to leave now, but I will be back. Do you work on Saturdays?" Edith was relieved to receive an affirmative nod. "I would like to hear the rest of the story. I will be back Saturday morning." Edith stood, smiled, and strode more purposefully out the front door than when she had come in. As she left, the tranquil door tone chimed once again, this time as if to say that joy was on the way.

CHAPTER 6

CAN YOU IMAGINE?

On Saturday at 8:58 a.m., Edith entered Marbles. This time, there was no hesitation in her steps and no question about what she wanted to order. She had money in hand and was ordering hot chocolate before she reached the counter.

She was eager to hear the rest of the story about Monica, but she was also excited to share her own story. Since her last visit, she had "found her own marble" and truly felt that she, like Monica, was beginning her journey out of the JZ. The marble she had received helped remind her to notice things for which she was grateful. She was amazed at how many good things happened to her everyday. She realized that she was nearly always healthy, even during the past flu season. Her bank account had enough money to cover her monthly expenses and then some. She had a happy, chubby cat that showed his affection by greeting her daily at the front door and by napping peacefully in her lap when she sat on the couch. And her job did not sound half as bad as Monica's! Edith realized that all these things had been there all along, but she had never noticed them.

The day after her first visit to Marbles, she had a flat tire on her way to work. Her initial instinct was to conclude that perhaps gratitude just wouldn't work for her. Who was she kidding? Rush hour was an awful time to have a flat tire. She had ended up waiting an hour and a half for help to arrive. After her tire was finally repaired, she was so frustrated, annoyed, and genuinely ungrateful, that she called in sick and returned home.

When she arrived home, she flipped on the television as usual and heard the report of the large multi-car accident. The accident had occurred on the Eisenhower Expressway, her exact route to work. Edith noted the time of the accident and calculated that she would have been at the accident scene almost exactly when it had happened had she not been delayed. She had never been more grateful for a flat tire.

Edith sat at the same table as her first visit. Marbles was not as busy today as it had been at the beginning of the week. She scanned Marbles and noticed her friend standing with an older man in the far corner of the store. The man first shook her hand then gave her a hug. She admired her new friend who seemed so graceful and elegant. She looked happy and at peace with the world.

As the man turned to leave, Edith's friend glanced around Marbles as if she knew someone was watching her. When their eyes met, Edith thought that she detected a look of pleasure in her new friend's eyes. She walked toward Edith and sat down.

Edith's story just gushed out. It felt good to share it with someone who listened. When she finished, Edith took a breath and said, "Please, tell me the rest of the story. What happened with Monica?"

"Where were we?"

"Earl," Edith replied. Her friend nodded and began.

 Dinnertime was different and they all knew it. Monica, Marnie, and Josh had started to eat dinner together more regularly. Monica had explained how eating dinner together was something that would bring joy into her life. She asked for their help and cooperation. At first, Marnie and Josh seemed hesitant, but neither of them could deny the sincerity of her request. And although neither of them would admit it, they could both see the change in their mom, and they liked it. Because they were more willing to spend time with her, they agreed to her plan. There was grumbling when they learned that helping to cook and clean was part of the deal, but they kept their commitment.

Monica had looked forward all week to her favorite dinner of chicken fajitas, fresh salsa with chips, and Mexican rice. It was Marnie's turn to help cook, so she sautéed green and red bell peppers and diced red onions while Monica sliced chicken breasts into thin strips. Remembering that there were tortillas warming in the oven, Monica asked Marnie to remove them. Marnie removed the plate and held it up, "Flour *and* corn—thanks, Mom." Monica smiled at Marnie but chuckled to herself as she thought of the past arguments over corn versus flour tortillas. How could two siblings have such strong opinions over soft tortillas *and* toilet paper?

At least they agreed that for two evenings a week, one would help prepare dinner and the other would load the dishwasher and help clean the kitchen. It was Josh's turn to help clean up. As Monica left the kitchen, Josh was recklessly sponging crumbs into the sink. He swiftly wiped the counter top, dropping more crumbs onto the floor than into the sink. Monica stopped to say something but held her tongue. The peace and cooperation her children were giving her was more important than a perfectly clean kitchen. Monica patted Josh on the back and said, "Thank you." She leaned in to kiss him on the check, but he recoiled in mock horror. They both laughed, but Monica thought that she saw a gleam of appreciation in his eyes.

As she climbed the stairs to take a quick shower, she reflected gratefully on the change that was moving quietly through her life. She thought of Conor with his messy red hair. She now realized that she had needed to learn gratitude from Conor first to prepare her for what was next. Without Conor, she would not have understood CiCi's message to find daily joy, and she couldn't have possibly applied Earl's message to turn down the noise.

As she walked down the hall past Marnie's room, she glanced absently through the slightly open door. Marnie was sitting cross-legged on the floor next to stacks of magazines with torn-out pages scattered all around her. The mess was such a contrast to the neatness that normally permeated Marnie's room that Monica stopped. Marnie had always been organized. Monica remembered when Marnie was ten years old how she had organized an entire display of key chains and pens in a department store while waiting for Monica to buy a birthday present for Josh's best friend. Impressed by her work, the department store manager had invited Marnie to come apply for a job when she was sixteen. Marnie had a flair for decorating and neatness that was beyond her years, and her room normally showed it.

Monica knocked softly and opened the door several more inches. Marnie looked up and read the inquisitive look on Monica's face. Motioning to all the torn-out pages, she said, "Ms. Hamilton's Social Studies class. I have to put together a 'vision board.'"

Monica replied, "A vision board?" "Yeah, I guess Ms. Hamilton saw a story on TV about vision boards, and so she did one years ago. She said it helped her in her life. Anyway, she thought it would be a good idea if we all did one. She's calling it a living experiment."

"Can you explain the assignment to me?" Monica asked curiously. Marnie put down a magazine and turned to face Monica. "Well, Ms. Hamilton said that your mind responds to things you see and how you feel when you see them. So we're all creating a poster with images of how we want our life to look in five years, and we'll present our posters in class next week. She says that the images help you attract things into your life because you focus attention on them. It's sort of like using your imagination to create your future, I guess."

Monica nodded thoughtfully. "So how are you using those magazines to help you imagine your life?" Monica was intrigued. Marnie explained, "Well, I took some fashion magazines that I had and asked dad last weekend if I could have some old magazines from his waiting room. So what I do is just start looking through magazines by flipping the pages. When I see an image that makes me feel good or that catches my eye, I tear it out. Ms. Hamilton said to go for volume first then choose your favorite images later. She said to think about different aspects of your life, like where you want to live, what you want to do, who you want to spend your time with, and what you want to look and feel like—stuff like that."

Picking two pictures out of the clutter, Marnie continued, "Remember the dance camp you sent me to a couple of summers ago in Colorado? Well, ever since then, I thought it would be cool to live by the mountains after I finish college. I found pictures of this place that is just like I imagined." Monica examined the first picture of a quaint bungalow with a wrap-around porch surrounded by towering pine trees, framed by grey, snow-capped mountains, blue sky, and a bubbling mountain stream. Holding up the second picture, Marnie said, "I can imagine myself right there with a Siberian Husky named 'Sophie.' I also want to make sure that I am still dancing or maybe even teaching dance classes, so I tore out that picture over there," she said pointing to a photo of a dancer in a classic pose.

Marnie continued, "I'm not sure if I want to have a serious boyfriend in five years, so I have pictures of cute guys but also groups of girls and guys just hanging out and laughing. That way if I do decide to date just one guy, there will be lots of cute guys in my future to choose from." Monica was amazed. Marnie made it all seem so simple. "You have put some serious thought into your images, Marnie," Monica complimented sincerely. Marnie nodded, "Ms. Hamilton said that the clearer you can state what you want and positively expect it all to show up, the quicker it will show up. It *is* a living experiment, right? And it is actually kind of fun.

"Ms. Hamilton told us about one of her girlfriends named Carrie who felt stuck in her job but didn't think that just changing jobs would be enough to get her unstuck, so she decided to dream bigger. She did a vision board that had a description of her ideal job and other stuff too. Three months later, she ran into a guy she used to work with and happened to tell him she was looking for a new job. He convinced his boss to interview Carrie even though they didn't have a job opening or money. During the interview, she wowed them by talking about what she could do for them. They ended up offering Carrie a job and told her to write up the job description she spoke about in the interview. All she had to do was get the job description off her vision board and send it to them. She wound up getting the exact job that she had created! Isn't that wild?"

Monica's breath caught in her throat as she suddenly realized that she was receiving a message from her daughter. She wanted more information but did not want to be a nosey mom. She asked nonchalantly, "So, how did the vision board help Ms. Hamilton?" "Oh, that was cool, too," Marnie said. "Ms. Hamilton said her vision board helped her to imagine herself healthy and travelling to far-away places, even though at the time, she was suffering from migraines and had not left the country in ten years. Since she made her vision board, her migraines have gotten better, and she's been to India and Australia. I thought this was kind of weird at first, but she said it is important to imagine what you want as if it were *already* happening—even to the point of imagining how you will feel. She said it helps if you get yourself in a happy mood because you can attract what you want faster when you are happy than if you are grumpy and focusing on negative things."

Monica felt an electric spark surge through her body and that familiar tingly feeling. That was it! Her next step was to imagine what she wanted. It all fit with the journey she was on. She sat down on the edge of Marnies' bed deep in thought. Her encounter with Conor showed her how gratitude could improve her life. The more she focused on what she was grateful for, the more things appeared in her life for which she could be grateful. Then she met CiCi on the train and learned that she should not delay opportunities to find joy on a daily basis. Everyday there were ways that she could find joy, like buying fresh-cut flowers, calling her college roommate Joyce instead of just exchanging Christmas cards, or finally taking off the ugly, dark blue blanket that covered her living room sofa.

She laughed to herself. She had originally put the blue blanket on the couch to save it from the inevitable crumbs, stains, and soda spills by her kids and their friends. But instead of preserving her beautiful leaf-patterned, beige couch, she had just covered it up. After meeting CiCi, she knew that seeing that couch everyday would bring her daily joy. The couch was the first piece of furniture Monica had purchased after her divorce, and it was something she had picked out by herself. Now, with the blue blanket taken off, the sofa beautified her living room and brought her joy—which was the reason she had bought it in the first place! She remembered thinking after removing the blanket that she had become a lot like her couch. She had covered herself for preservation and protection. But the very act of covering up had stifled her authentic self.

Was it a coincidence that the next person to help her in her journey out of the JZ was Earl with his deep, gravelly voice and his cool grey hat? From Earl she had learned to turn down the noise and tune in the peace. Monica had learned that when she was able to immerse herself in silence, she could hear her inner voice speaking more clearly to her mind. She smiled at the thought of Earl and made a mental note to thank him again for his wisdom.

She had decided to turn down the noise by turning off noisy things and by meditating each day. At first, making time just to sit silently in mindful reflection—letting her thoughts wander without judgement or attempts to solve problems—was very frustrating for Monica. Her thoughts sometimes wandered so far off the beaten path that she feared she would have to send out a search party! Once she found herself thinking about a jelly-bean eating contest in the sixth grade and wondered where her mind stored all those memories! That wasn't so bad, though. Early on in her attempt to turn down the noise, her mind would sometimes wander to places that were not healing. On a particularly bad rant of self-loathing, she found herself overanalyzing and critiquing her mistakes that had contributed to her broken relationship. But, like anything new, the more she relaxed in the process and let it unfold rather than trying to control or corral her thoughts, the more she enjoyed the beautiful silence. At first, it seemed like an eternity before the oven timer signalled that fifteen minutes was up, but now it seemed to pass too quickly. Regardless, she had noticed that her attention and ability to focus on tasks seemed to be better after her silent time. Most important, a consistent peaceful feeling was beginning to take root in her heart.

Now, her own fifteen-year-old daughter was teaching her something that her intuition sensed was another way-point on her journey. Monica needed clarity on what she wanted her ideal life to look like and feel like. Just like Marnie, she could create clarity with her imagination by building her own vision board. "Vision board," she mumbled. She liked the way that sounded. She tried to remember when she had last allowed herself to dream. It had been a long time.

"Did you say something, Mom?" Marnie asked. Composing herself, Monica said, "Vision board…what a great idea. Because sometimes people can get so busy just existing that there is no energy left to dream." Marnie paused then asked, "But if you don't allow yourself to dream, wouldn't you find yourself living out someone else's dreams?" Monica ran her fingers through Marnie's long, dark ponytail and pulled the end in a playful tug, "How did I get such a wise daughter?" she questioned to no one in particular. "That's easy," Marnie retorted. "I eat corn instead of flour tortillas!" They both laughed.

Monica left Marnie's room and walked down the hall to her own bedroom. She could see that it would take some work actually to think about what kind of life she really wanted now and in her future. She wouldn't have had the initial energy, perspective, or ability to focus to escape the JZ if she had tried to imagine her future or build a vision board as a first step. All the prior steps were important and necessary. She felt ready to try a vision board for herself. So, she picked up a magazine from her bedside table and reached into a top dresser drawer for a small pair of scissors she often used to cut off the tags from new clothes. Monica smiled as she remembered being grateful months ago for opposable thumbs. At that moment, she could not have been any more grateful.

 Something suddenly clicked in Edith's head. She whirled around and looked at the artwork on the walls. She turned back and with excitement in her voice exclaimed, "Those are vision boards! I thought they were just collages, but they are vision boards!" Her discovery was affirmed by a quiet nod. "Excuse me!" Edith said as she stood quickly, nearly tipping over her chair. She studied several of them before returning to the table. Her eyes sparkled with the joy of her discovery, and she announced, "Of course, of course! Now I understand. They're *perfect* in here." Eager to hear the rest of the story, Edith said, "Please continue."

CHAPTER 7

CONNECT WITH SUPPORT

It took Monica three weeks to create her vision board. She had collected a large stack of images from magazines the night Marnie had introduced her to the vision board concept. But she felt she needed to develop a clearer internal vision before she arranged her images on a vision board. Placing the images on the board felt like a serious commitment, and she wanted to make sure she got it right.

So she dug out the barely used, red leather journal she had purchased after her divorce and wrote words that described how she wanted to feel: happy, vibrant, useful, abundant, healthy, alive, and loved. Most important, she connected her desired feelings with a powerful motive. She wanted quietly to make the world a better place by helping others find their way out of the JZ.

Monica noticed that when she thought about her desired feelings and considered her underlying motive, she experienced a peaceful resonance in her heart. She believed that this feeling confirmed that she was headed in the right direction. She knew the words were right for her because they described the person she passionately wanted to become. So, she wrote her seven words on two, large Post-It notes and stuck one on her dresser mirror and the other on her computer monitor at work. Looking at her words daily helped Monica focus on the feelings she wanted to have in her life. In her heart, Monica also knew that she needed a vision board. She sensed that a vision board would help her *see* how all of those feelings could become manifested.

After several days of mental processing, Monica finally decided to commit to a vision board. She started with a sturdy poster board, purchased at an office supply store she often passed on her lunchtime walks. She chose one with a deep blue background because the color made her feel peaceful.

Monica wanted to place the vision board in her home where she would see it during quiet moments. She felt that the vision would have the best chance to find its way into her heart when she was reflective. It did not take her long to find the perfect spot. She placed her blank vision board on a telephone stand in her bedroom and leaned it against the wall so she could see it in the morning when she awoke and at night before she went to sleep. Having the background for the vision board was a start; now she just needed to choose and arrange her images.

During her walks and morning meditation, her larger vision had taken shape. She knew three things for certain. First, she loved Chicago. She loved the pace, the faces, the culture, the lake, the food, and the art. She loved everything about Chicago. She especially enjoyed the four seasons. She giggled to herself as she thought about a forwarded email from Marty. "Chicago has two seasons: winter and construction!" She laughed again. She had really evolved if she remembered and enjoyed emails from Marty. There was no question about it; Monica would stay in Chicago.

Second, she loved her children, and before they moved away from home, she wanted to spend the precious time she had left, teaching and modeling the principles she had been learning. Monica wanted to prepare Marnie and Josh for life so they would know how to be grateful and find daily joy. Mostly, she wanted to inoculate them against the JZ.

Lastly, she knew that finding a different way to support her family was absolutely essential. Her job was becoming more and more draining in every imaginable way. Ironically, she found her co-workers much easier to deal with the more she evolved as a person. She felt good about helping Cynthia through a small crisis and for actually going to visit Marty in his office. She had changed, and that had affected her way of relating with others. So, it wasn't the people; it was *clearly* the work.

More than once, she found herself doodling financial notes on a dinner napkin. Her brain was churning, and her heart was preparing her for something else, but for what? Not knowing where to start, she had called an acquaintance who worked in small business financing. He talked her through all the typical steps of start-up. It was a helpful conversation, but she didn't come away with any definite answers. However, she *did* have a strong sense that she was about to become a small business owner.

She knew that to be consistent with her true purpose, her business had to be about more than just making money. Somehow, it had to improve the lives of her customers. The accountant in her eventually came to accept the idea that helping others could be a viable business model. When Monica envisioned herself in a store of her own, the evolving Monica felt happy, alive, and useful, but the accountant Monica felt a little apprehensive. Still, she knew that it was time to commit her images to the vision board.

Monica placed a unique photo of the Chicago skyline in the center of her vision board. Its uniqueness stemmed from the fact that it had not been taken from the lake or one of the buildings commonly used for so many postcard photos. Instead, it had been taken from a building somewhere west of the city and gave an entirely different view. Something about this scene made her feel peaceful. She didn't know why, but she really liked the photo.

She also included wallet-sized photos of Marnie and Josh on her board. She always wanted her children to be part of her life even if they didn't live in Chicago. She included images of a backyard flower garden with a pond, a woman sitting in a meadow painting a landscape, a serene, healthy-looking woman doing yoga, a Christmas mug filled with hot chocolate and topped by a perfect whipped cream swirl with chocolate shavings, and a happy-looking couple riding bicycles on a country road.

She developed the habit of studying her vision board several times a day. Gradually, the images became familiar and settled deeper into her mind and heart. After a couple of weeks, she noticed that a flower shop had become one of her new favorite stops when she left the office. She connected her growing interest in flowers with her vision board the day she began sketching a new design for her backyard that included a small pond surrounded by a flower garden. It excited her when she realized that this was the first manifestation that her vision board experiment was working.

It didn't surprise her much a month later when she spontaneously pulled off the freeway into an art shop she had never noticed before and purchased some painting supplies or when she signed up to take a Yoga class with Marnie. She even came to understand that the photo of the happy couple on bicycles suggested a growing openness to try another relationship. Eventually, she came to expect that everything on her vision board would eventually manifest. So it was only natural that she grew increasingly curious to learn how the image of the Chicago skyline and the mug of hot chocolate would play into her future.

 One chilly fall morning, Monica studied her vision board before leaving her bedroom. She had discovered that stopping long enough to carefully study each of the images on her vision board was an important daily ritual. On this particular morning, her eyes were drawn to the image of the hot chocolate. As the seasons changed and the weather turned cooler, she had developed a craving for a good cup of hot chocolate. She laughed to herself as she wondered whether this vision board stuff was really about subliminal advertising. She was, after all, having a very powerful craving!

She stopped at the top of the stairs to reflect on a memory of the best cup of hot chocolate she had ever had. It was in Europe with her college roommate Joyce, the summer before her senior year at the University of Illinois. She and Joyce had roomed together for Monica's last two years of college. During that time, they became inseparable, lifelong friends. Monica still felt that Joyce was among her closest friends even though they had been out of touch for the past few years.

Monica smiled as she remembered how they had met. After her second year in college, Monica was ready to move out of the dorms. She had found Joyce's name and number on a message board posted at the student union. The ad was handwritten on yellow notebook paper with flowers drawn in blue pen all around the phone number. Monica was studying business with an accounting minor, and to her knowledge, none of her classmates had ever drawn flowers on anything! She guessed that the person who posted the ad was a carefree spirit who would provide a welcome contrast to her current reality. Monica removed the notice and called that day. The two hit it off immediately, and Monica had moved in by the end of the week.

In so many ways, Monica and Joyce were polar opposites. Monica had dark curly hair and hazel eyes. Joyce was tall with light green eyes and long, straight blond hair. Monica was somewhat shy while Joyce was extraverted and gregarious. Monica was studious and focused on her education while Joyce focused on her social life and often did not know where her textbooks were. But both of them loved to laugh, dance, and travel.

When their first year as roommates was nearly over, Joyce's father called with a surprise. He had won two, round-trip plane tickets to France through a contest at work. He didn't want to go, but he offered the tickets to Joyce and Monica. Because Joyce had an uncle who lived just outside of Paris, that meant a free trip and a free place to stay! They did not have to think twice before accepting the tickets. They spent two unforgettable weeks in France. The trip had cemented a sisterhood between them. They had so much fun dancing, sightseeing, and eating real food at local cafés. Monica remembered the hot chocolate she had had on their last night in Paris. It had spoiled her for life. She had never been able to find another cup that good.

A slamming bathroom door brought Monica back to reality. *Marnie must be up*, she thought. She decided that she would get a cup of hot chocolate before going in to work. She wondered what Joyce would say about her vision board and her growing interest in starting a business. *Only one way to find out*, Monica thought as she picked up the phone to call Joyce. Joyce picked up on the first ring. "Monica? I have been thinking about you for a week! I am so glad you called! So, tell me, girl friend, why have I been thinking about you?" Not waiting for an answer, Joyce continued, "Do you want to have some coffee this morning? I have time today."

Monica instantly thought of the little coffee shop across from her favorite park. She gave Joyce directions, and they agreed to meet later that morning. Monica called the office to tell them she would be a little late to work. She went back to her room to pull the hot chocolate image off her vision board. As an after thought, she also removed the image of the Chicago skyline. She put both images between the pages of her planner and said goodbye to Marnie through the bathroom door. As Monica walked through the kitchen on her way out, Josh saluted her with his spoon and said goodbye before he buried his face in his bowl of cereal.

Joyce saw Monica first and waved her over to a table by the window. Standing to embrace Monica, Joyce exclaimed, "Wow, Monica, you look great!" With hands on her hips and mock suspicion in her voice, Joyce said, "Something is *different* about you since we last got together!" Monica smiled and replied, "Let's order and I'll tell you all about it." Joyce paused dramatically then announced, "I already ordered. I got you a cup of hot chocolate with whipped cream! Do you remember that cup we had in France? You couldn't stop talking about it for weeks!"

Monica stood speechless. The feeling she had felt when she learned lessons from Conor and CiCi swept over her again. She had learned to recognize that feeling as a sign that she needed to pay attention. She was sure she had not said anything to Joyce about hot chocolate. Joyce asked, "Are you alright, Mon?" Monica sat down and took Joyce's hand. Monica said, looking into Joyce's eyes, "I am so good, Joyce. I am really, really good."

Joyce was completely absorbed by Monica's story. She questioned Monica as if she, too, was trying to learn about the principles that were helping Monica escape the JZ. Monica pulled the two images out of her planner to illustrate the vision board. Joyce looked at the picture of hot chocolate and asked, "By the way, how was your hot chocolate?" Monica sighed, "Not as good as that cup in France." Joyce laughed, "It never is."

Joyce handed the hot chocolate photo back to Monica and asked, "So what are you going to do, Mon?" Monica shrugged and replied, "I don't know, but I think I am supposed to leave my job and start a business." "What kind of business?" asked Joyce. Monica tapped her index finger on her cup of nearly full hot chocolate, "I'm not sure about the 'what' but I feel that I need to help other people somehow. Of course, I also need to support my family." Joyce nodded, "Yeah—the kids will be in college before you know it, and that's expensive." Monica nodded, fully aware of the financial reality that eight-plus years of college would bring.

There was a reflective lull in the conversation. Joyce broke the silence. "Monica, listen to me. I'm your friend. You always had a great head for business and crunching numbers. But this does not sound like a normal business you are talking about here. This is big. This is life changing." Joyce touched Monica's hand. "You are going to need some support while you find that 'something' you are passionate about. Why don't we meet a couple of times a month? I would love to support you. It will probably help me, too!"

A wave of understanding swept over Monica, and she nodded. So *that* is why she had thought of calling Joyce. She needed the support that Joyce had to offer. Anyone following her true purpose would need support from positive friends. That had to be the next step. *Connect with support,* she thought to herself. She looked at Joyce and knew that she would not get better support from anyone. Monica said,

"I think that's a great idea. We should get together a few times a month."

But Joyce didn't respond. She hadn't heard Monica. She had pulled the image of the Chicago skyline out of Monica's planner and was studying it. Her eyes were scanning the image from side to side, and her mouth was moving, but nothing was coming out. Suddenly, her eyes grew wide, and a smile erupted across her face. Monica asked, "What is it Joyce?"

Showing the image to Monica, Joyce replied, "I think I know where this photo was taken. It was one of my favorite places when I was a kid. Do you remember Uncle Brad from France?" Monica nodded. Joyce continued, "When I was a kid, Uncle Brad and Aunt Doreen took my brother and me to get pancakes every so often on Saturday mornings. There was this quaint breakfast diner tucked in an old brick building. And I remember a cute little bakery next door where we would stop to get cinnamon rolls for later." Joyce laughed, "That is what Uncle Brad said, but he always ate his cinnamon roll before we got to the train station." Joyce looked at the image again. She shook her head and smiled. "I have such great memories of that place. Sometimes we would climb up to the roof after breakfast and just look at Chicago. I think the building was only three or four stories high. This picture looks as if it was taken from the roof or pretty close to it." She looked at the image again and recalled, "Aunt Doreen always said that Chicago was the greatest place on earth." She let out a soft sigh as the memories came flooding back. "Then Uncle Brad got transferred to Paris."

Sitting upright, Joyce gushed, "Mon, I have a great idea! Why don't you bring the kids, and we'll all go to get pancakes this Saturday morning? It'll be fun!" Monica thought about getting Marnie and Josh out of bed early enough on Saturday to have a meal before noon. She didn't want to push her luck by disturbing the teenager karma. Home felt more peaceful these days, and she didn't want to disrupt that. She explained, "We tend to sleep late on Saturdays, Joyce. I don't think pancakes would be enough to pull Josh out of bed unless they were served at 2 p.m. Let me think about it—I hate to disrupt the rhythm we're in. The kids are pretty happy these days."

"All right, Mon—just call me if you change your mind." Joyce looked at her watch and stood to leave. She leaned in and kissed Monica on the cheek. "See you Saturday morning," she teased. Joyce strode to the door where she paused to sweep her long blonde mane out of her face and pull her silk shawl over her shoulders. She stepped out into the breezy fall morning and seemed to float out the door and down the street in her own lively rhythm. All eyes were on her as she exited the coffee shop. *Classic Joyce*, thought Monica. She could make an entrance *and* an exit better than anyone she knew.

CHAPTER 8

DO SOMETHING YOU
HAVE NEVER DONE

Monica took a few moments to gather herself after Joyce's dramatic departure. She felt more certain of her decision to start a business, but she still could not see the details. What could she do that would provide a meaningful way to support her family? When should she quit her job? She had so many questions. She shook her head. She knew she needed to be patient and just let it come to her. Everything else had.

She left the coffee shop and stepped outside into the brisk autumn air. As if by habit, she looked across the street towards the park. She loved that place. It was her sanctuary. There were fewer people in the park now that the temperature had cooled. But her heart skipped a beat when she saw Earl. *That guy never misses a day*, she thought. *No wonder he always has a smile on his face.* Monica looked at her watch. She was running late, but she didn't care. She felt compelled to cross the street to talk to Earl.

Earl saw Monica coming halfway across the park and raised one hand in a wave of recognition. She smiled and returned the wave. As she approached Earl, she asked, "Mind if I sit down?" He smiled. "Not at all, dear lady," he said, motioning to the empty space next to him as he moved his grey hat, "by all means."

"I am Monica Montoya," she said extending her hand. Earl took her hand and squeezed firmly. "Early Duprey, but my friends call me Earl. The pleasure is mine," he said bowing his head.

"Early…that is an interesting name. There must be a story there somewhere," Monica said with a smile. Earl laughed his wonderful deep, raspy laugh. "Supposed to be born on New Year's Day, but I came two weeks early." He held up two fingers to emphasize the point. "When the nurse handed me to my mama, she said 'Ain't he early?' I been early ever since." He laughed again at his own humor. He paused for a moment and continued, "You been coming here for a while. What's on your mind?" Earl paused and examined her face.

Monica smiled and said, "You're right, Earl. I am a park regular. And on my mind is a burning question for you." Earl looked surprised. His face suggested that he expected to ask the questions. He repeated, "You have a question for me?"

Monica turned herself on the bench so she could see Earl's face and said, "I do." She waited a few moments to make sure she had his approval and full attention. The look on his face indicated that he was enjoying his new role of "man with all the answers." Monica continued, "A few weeks back, I was eating my lunch right over there." She motioned to the bench behind them. "And you were having a conversation with your friend about cinnamon rolls." Earl's face went blank for a moment then he tipped his head back and roared. Monica had never heard such a hearty laugh. He held nothing back at all. It was like a force of nature spilling out into the autumn air—a fully authentic, belly laugh, and it was infectious. Monica soon started laughing, too.

Earl let out one last bellow and a hoot then removed his handkerchief to wipe the corners of his eyes. He looked at Monica, his eyes and mouth still threatening to explode in laughter and said, "That fool Ellis." He shook his head. "I never met anyone who argues like Ellis. He had a cinnamon roll in Cincinnati a few months back. He was there visiting his family. He told me he had the best cinnamon roll ever made. Went on and on about it. Now, I know that can't be true because I *know* cinnamon rolls," he said, waving his finger in the air for emphasis. "And I know where they make the best cinnamon roll, and it is right here in Chicago! They been makin' 'em for over eighty years, and I get one every Monday for breakfast."

He held up his fist and exclaimed, "They're bigger than my fist, and they have lots of thin layers so they are never too doughy. When you take a bite, they melt in your mouth. They have butter on 'em instead of that fake stuff, brown not white sugar, and not too much cinnamon. Cinnamon gets caught in my throat," he explained, touching his neck. "And you can get 'em with walnuts or pecans, but they never, *ever* have raisins. Cinnamon rolls aren't supposed to have raisins," he said, motioning with his hands and raising his voice as if he was giving a sermon. "I like the pecans," he added as an afterthought. "And they come swimmin' in a creamy frosting that ain't too sweet or heavy. Cinnamon rolls with heavy, sweet frosting are tryin' to hide something. And you can't eat 'em with your hands; you gotta use a fork." Then he said with finality, "And Ellis don't know nothin' about cinnamon rolls!"

Monica was amused by Earl's passion over something as simple as a cinnamon roll, but just the same, she felt her mouth beginning to water. She was contemplating whether to ask Earl about other topics that he and Ellis had debated or to ask him where to find this coveted cinnamon roll. But Earl solved the dilemma for her. "You like cinnamon rolls?" he asked. Monica nodded. "You oughta get one of these cinnamon rolls. They sell 'em at a bakery that's pretty close to the Oak Park station. The bakery's in a three-story brick building that has been there for a hundred years or so. Used to be a little breakfast place next door, but they closed about a year back."

The skin on Monica's arms began to tingle. Could it be that Earl was describing the same building that Joyce had just described? Could it be the same building from her vision board image? Practically everything else from her vision board had been manifested. Earl interrupted her thoughts, "You should go get one of those cinnamon rolls, Monica. You know, sometimes it's good to try something you've never done before. Do it while you're young before you get set in your ways like me," he said with a gleam in his eyes.

Monica's heart skipped a beat. She jumped up and nearly shouted, "That's right. I need to do something I have never done before! New thinking leads to new actions, and new actions lead to new results. Of course! Why didn't I see it before?" Earl looked confused. He was not used to anyone taking his advice so literally and quickly. Monica sat down again and touched his arm. "I'm sorry Earl. You just told me something that I really needed to hear. I will do something I have never done before. I will go have the best cinnamon roll in Chicago this Saturday morning with or without my kids!"

Monica gave Earl a look of gratitude. "Thank you, Earl, for answering my question and for…answering my question." Earl, still a little confused, just nodded his head and said, "Obliged, my dear, much obliged." Suddenly, Monica felt an indescribable clarity, as though her thoughts and feelings were perfectly aligned. She felt this clarity resonate throughout her body and heard an inner voice that quietly whispered, "Yes." Both Earl and Joyce had helped Monica form a clear vision of what she really wanted. She finally knew the business she would own, and she had a pretty good idea where it would be located.

Edith was spellbound. She was sitting in Marbles, surrounded by vision boards, and listening to the most amazing story she had ever heard. She had so many questions. Finally, she could not contain herself any longer so she asked, "What happened to Earl?"

"Earl." There was a momentary pause. "Earl passed last year. We took flowers and cinnamon rolls to his funeral. After all, Marbles sells the best cinnamon rolls in Chicago!" Edith stared incredulously. All of a sudden, it made sense to her, and she exclaimed pointing across the table, "You are Monica! Oh my gosh! You are Monica! I should have seen it!" Her friend flashed a smile and teased, "No, I am not Monica, but this story is my story, too, and now it is your story. Perhaps I should formally introduce myself. Edith, I am Joyce."

Edith's jaw dropped. Joyce continued, "My life was also transformed by Monica's vision. I have been her friend through her search for the best cup of hot chocolate since that night in Paris, and now she makes it right here at Marbles. How could I refuse her invitation to join her in this business? Besides, none of this is really about warm pastries and hot beverages, now is it? It is about helping people like you, Edith."

Edith's mouth began to tremble. At first all she could say was "Joyce." Then tears began to well up, and she managed, "Nobody...nobody has ever spent time with me like this...." Her voice broke. "Thank you," she whispered as she began to sob quietly. Joyce paused a moment then leaned across the table to touch Edith's hand. "Would you like to hear the rest of the story?" Edith nodded emphatically. Joyce paused with a sly grin and continued, "Do you think we should ask Monica to bring us a cinnamon roll with two forks?"

Her eyes now wide open, Edith looked up at Joyce. She whipped her head around to scan the faces behind the counter. Her eyes fell upon a gentle, gracious face framed by dark curly hair. Edith looked back at Joyce with a question in her eyes. Joyce nodded her head. "That is Monica." Edith, her eyes glistening with grateful tears, was fighting back a flood of emotions. She rose and walked slowly toward Monica.

Monica saw Edith coming and stepped from behind the counter to meet her. Edith didn't know what to say. She fumbled for the right words, "The story...it's you! I mean, you're

Monica, and your story...you started Marbles!" Monica smiled then looked around, "This is the business I was supposed to start, and this is the kind of hug I am supposed to give." The two embraced. Edith could no longer contain herself. She began to sob as if all of the sadness and sorrow was draining out of her in a flood. Monica held Edith and said nothing. She just let Edith cry. Nobody in Marbles seemed to mind.

When Edith regained her composure, Monica said tenderly, "This story now includes you, Edith. Would you like to hear the rest of it? Wiping her eyes, Edith nodded. Monica walked her back to the table and sat down next to her. Joyce handed Edith a tissue and looked at Monica with a twinkle in her eye, "I can't continue this story without a cinnamon roll, Monica!" Monica smiled at Joyce and Edith as she stood to fill her friend's request. "I'll be right back," she said, motioning for Joyce to continue the story. Joyce had related the story of Marbles so many times that, out of habit, she picked up where she had left off as if Edith didn't know the identity of the characters.

 Joyce woke up with a start as she heard her phone ringing. She looked over at the bedside clock radio in disbelief. It was ten after seven on Saturday morning, for crying out loud! She contemplated covering her head with a pillow but didn't. "Hello," she said, trying to sound as if she had been up for hours. "Joyce," Monica blurted, "meet me at nine for breakfast." Joyce rubbed her left eye with her free hand and protested, "Mon, do you know what time...?" Monica interrupted, "Joyce, we have to go get cinnamon rolls at that bakery, the one next to the little diner you told me about. And, we have to do it today!" Monica had an urgent tone that Joyce hadn't heard since college. Joyce could tell this was important. "Okay, Mon, I can meet you at nine," she said as she slid out of bed. "Wait! Did I tell you where this place is?" asked Joyce. "I have directions. I'll see you there at nine," Monica said as she hung up the phone.

As she dried her hair and applied her weekend make-up routine of eyeliner and lipstick, Monica felt exhilarated. For the first time in years, she felt as if she was on a path that she was meant to follow. Everything just felt right. Her kids were still sleeping when she left, so she wrote them a quick note. She would explain everything to them later. Monica could feel that something big was going to happen this morning, something that she had been unknowingly anticipating throughout her journey out of the JZ. Her intuition told her this would not be the time to be distracted by grumpy teenagers.

The train seemed to take forever before finally arriving at the Oak Park station. Monica smiled to herself as she remembered observing the way that people tried to get on and off the train at the same time during the work week. But on Saturday, it was more relaxed. There were more families with small children. The excited giggles and restlessness of the children were perfectly in tune with Monica's mood.

She looked at her watch. *Good*, she thought, *I'm still early*. She wanted to get to the bakery before Joyce. Joyce didn't know that the diner was closed. Monica wanted to be there to break the news and to fill her in on her conversation with Earl.

She exited the train station and walked down through the cement tunnel to the street. She turned left as she exited the station. Earl had told her that the bakery was two blocks east of the station. She turned and walked briskly. She was surprised by how many people were out walking, running, or shopping. She liked the way the area felt. It was vibrant and alive. She stopped to examine her surroundings. She was one block from the train station. There were residential buildings to the north and east. There was a park a few blocks away; she could see the trees.

Somewhere, not too far away, she could hear the sound of an alto saxophone humming a careless melody that sounded as if it were being spontaneously composed. Her heart began to pound in anticipation, and she started walking again, this time a bit more quickly. It seemed that all of her senses were heightened. She took a deep breath. The wind was swirling in mild fall gusts. It felt cool and refreshing. She brushed her hair out of her eyes and tipped her face up to the sun. It was unusually pleasant for a fall day in Chicago.

She noticed that she was getting closer to the saxophone. She crossed the street and noted that she had just walked two blocks. She moved to the edge of the sidewalk to get a better angle, scanning ahead for a three-story building. Just then, the most glorious smell tickled her nose. It was the unmistakeable smell of fresh cinnamon rolls! She knew she was close.

She reached the source of the smell in a few minutes. The bakery was located on a corner in a free-standing, brick building. The top two floors appeared to be apartments, but the bottom floor was commercial. The bakery was on the right nearest the corner, and the diner had been next door to the left. There was a flat green sign on the door of the diner that said, "Closed. Thank you for your business."

Monica stepped back into the street to get a better perspective. The building was old, but it was full of charm and had been beautifully renovated. The windows on the second and third floors protruded, and the roofline had elegant accents. *They don't make buildings like this anymore,* thought Monica. But there was something else. There was a special feeling connected with this building. Monica felt as if she had come home. Standing there in front of that building was the culmination of many events involving many different people. She thought how amazing it was that she had selected a photo taken from this building on her way out of the JZ. Somehow it represented the recognition of a dream. She felt a familiar lump in her throat. She was overwhelmed. She did not know what role this building would play in her life, but somehow she just knew, deep inside, that it signalled her final step out of the joyless zone.

A honking horn brought her out of her reverie. She dashed to the safety of the sidewalk and turned her attention to the building once again. On the far left side of the building, she noticed a young woman in her early twenties exiting a door with a small white dog on a leash. Monica moved toward the door. The young woman stopped and re-entered the building as if she had forgotten something. Monica reached the door and waited for the young woman. Within minutes the door swung open again, and the dog bounced through the doorway followed by the young woman. Monica waited until they cleared the doorway then caught the door.

She entered the building and let her eyes adjust to the light. There was a small lobby with mailboxes on her left and an elevator on her right. It had a hinged metal door instead of the modern sliding stainless steel doors. She could see and hear the elevator as it approached the first floor. The elevator looked and sounded old. Just beyond the elevator was a white and grey marble staircase with metal railings. Monica chose the stairs. She climbed quickly up the first four sets of stairs. Each flight covered half a floor then turned back 180 degrees. Stopping to catch her breath, she examined the well-used steps. The center of each was worn and discolored. *How many feet*, Monica wondered, *have walked up and down these marble steps over the years?*

Monica continued upward to the top of the stairs and found the door that led to the rooftop. She propped it open with one of the rocks just outside the door and walked out onto the rooftop balcony, pausing a moment to take it all in. There was a protective border around the edge of the roof with an iron fence mounted on top. To her left, there were some pots that held the last of the summer's tomato plants. Two small green tomatoes still clung to the dried up vine. These tomatoes would not get the chance to ripen. A gold and blue striped hammock hung on Monica's right, cleverly suspended between the second rung of the fire escape ladder and a brace that secured the iron fence to the building.

Monica moved toward the edge of the roof. The aroma of cinnamon rolls wafting upwards once again tickled her nose. She took a deep breath and closed her eyes. There was nothing artificial about that smell. She opened her eyes and looked at the view of the city's skyline. She smiled. She couldn't believe it. The view was exactly the perspective that was captured in her vision board photo. This view had become part of her subconscious. She felt a wave of appreciation sweep through her body as she reflected on all the synchronicities that had come into her life to lead her to this place in this moment. With fondness, she recalled the people who were part of her story: Conor, CiCi, Marnie, Earl, and Joyce.

"Joyce!" she exclaimed out loud. She had forgotten about Joyce! Monica wanted to meet her before she got to the diner so she could tell her the whole story. She rushed back across the roof top, through the door, and down the stairs. Once outside, her eyes focused on the faces of the pedestrians walking down the street. There she was! Joyce was strolling toward Monica as if she owned the sidewalk. Her hair was pulled back in a ponytail, and she was wearing faded blue jeans, cowboy boots, with a brown leather jacket over a pink button-down shirt.

Joyce spoke first, "Isn't that smell glorious? Just as I remember…." Her voice trailed off as she noticed the closed sign on the door of the diner. Monica took Joyce by the arm and pulled her in to the bakery and said, "The diner is closed, Joyce. I'll fill you in. But first, I really need one of those cinnamon rolls!"

Joyce listened with undivided attention as Monica related her encounter with Earl. She explained how Earl had identified this bakery as the home of the best cinnamon roll in Chicago and how she had learned that the diner was closed. Joyce was annoyed, and her wrinkled brow and pinched eyebrows showed it. "I don't understand how that diner could go out of business. It was always busy from breakfast through lunch for years!" she exclaimed dramatically. "That is exactly why it is closed," said a male voice from behind the counter. Monica and Joyce looked around to see a tall, blond man with bright, blue eyes wiping his calloused hands on a dough-caked apron. "I am sorry to interrupt, but you were expecting to find a diner that has been closed. I apologize to you, miss, but my wife and I are the ones who closed it." "But why?" asked Joyce. "It was always so busy!"

"Perhaps I should introduce myself. I am Stefan," he said, while removing his apron. He continued, "My grandparents opened this bakery not long after they came from Sweden in the early 1920's. They arrived in Chicago without much except each other and a great recipe for cinnamon rolls. They opened the diner about ten years after the bakery because they wanted a place where they could sell their bakery items and they wanted their children to learn the value of hard work.

"You are right. It was very popular. It was open for three generations, but in the end, it became to too much for my wife and me to manage. I am the only one in my family left in the bakery business. Both my brothers work in the city, and my sister lives in Florida. My wife and I decided that we needed to simplify our lives and our business, so we closed the diner over a year ago." Looking at Joyce, he said, "I am sorry. You were looking forward to eating there today, and we have disappointed you." His smile was warm and engaging, his eyes tired but sincere. "We are concentrating on baked goods, especially the best cinnamon roll in Chicago," he said with a twinkle in his eye.

Monica spontaneously pushed out a chair, inviting Stefan to join them. The store was busy, but most of the action seemed to be coming from the back. Stefan noticed Monica studying his workers and came to the same conclusion, so he sat down. He volunteered, "Most of our business these days is direct delivery of our product to other bakeries and restaurants. We want to expand that part of our business, but we are not sure how." Monica asked, "Is the empty space next door part of your expansion plans?" Studying Monica's face, Stefan paused for a moment. Sensing her honest intent, he continued, "No, we own that space and the bakery outright, so we don't really need to use that space. The challenge is that we want to honor the legacy of my grandparents by running a retail establishment next door, but we just don't want to do it ourselves anymore. I cannot bring myself to sell the space or to do anything else besides what my grandfather envisioned." Pausing for a moment, he added, "My grandfather was such an amazing man. I wish that everyone today could have such a mentor."

A timer chimed from somewhere in the back of the bakery, and Stefan sighed deeply then clapped his hands together. "That is my cue," he said as he pushed back his chair and stood up. "If you will excuse me, ladies, there is work to be done and hot chocolate to make." Joyce and Monica looked at each other—their wide eyes sharing a conversation that went unspoken. At the same time, they both said, "We'll take two cups." They all laughed.

CHAPTER 9

GIVE BACK

Monica returned several times to the bakery to visit with Stefan and his wife, Jenna, and to enjoy the best hot chocolate she had found since that cup all those years ago in Paris. Eventually Stefan and Jenna revealed their deepest desire regarding the space next door. They wanted to create a warm, relaxing setting where people could escape the hustle and bustle of the world and connect with one another. On one visit, Stefan told Monica, "In my heart, I can see my grandfather in that space, helping and loving everyone who walked through the front door."

Together, Stefan and Monica decided that a coffee shop rather than a diner would allow a slower pace and would help create the atmosphere that Stefan and Jenna desired. Stefan also wanted their cinnamon rolls to be one of the featured items on the menu, and he insisted that they be priced fairly. He wanted people to know that the bakery next door could provide amazing cinnamon rolls for any store, restaurant, or event.

In the end, the arrangement worked perfectly. Stefan and his wife offered Monica rental terms that were reasonable. They trusted that Monica's vision was consistent with theirs and would preserve the legacy of Stefan's grandparents.

Monica loved Stefan's hot chocolate, but she came to realize that creating a signature hot chocolate recipe was something she would have to do on her own. She used Stefan's recipe as a starting point but chose a darker chocolate base and added cinnamon along with a couple other secret ingredients. It took her weeks of experimentation until she perfected the recipe. When she finally finished, Monica knew she would be offering a cup of hot chocolate worthy of the best cinnamon roll in Chicago.

She thought of Earl and chuckled. Between the two of them, they would know more about the featured menu items than anyone. After all, nobody knew more about cinnamon rolls than Earl, and she had learned an awful lot about hot chocolate! She could not wait to tell him that the diner would soon be opening but, this time, as a coffee shop. He would be the first person she would invite to the open house. It took about a year to make all the necessary arrangements to open her coffee shop. Most of that time was spent convincing Joyce that she should stop working in her husband's medical practice and join Monica in this life-changing venture. Joyce finally agreed about eight months after their first trip to the bakery. Even though Joyce was not stuck in the JZ, when she had started following the principles that Monica had discovered, she found that her life was transforming for the better.

Ultimately, the change in her own life convinced her to take the leap of faith and join Monica as a partner.

About three months before the opening, Monica was still undecided about the name of the coffee shop. One Saturday afternoon, Monica took her children and some of their friends to help finish painting. Josh and his friends painted the last two inside walls when Marnie came up with the idea of framing vision boards and hanging them on the wall as art. Back at home, she framed Monica's first, then her own. She asked some of her friends from Ms. Hamilton's class if they would donate their vision boards as well. A few of her friends helped Marnie put the frames together.

Marnie also came up with the idea of fresh flowers on each table. She had found some blue glass vases at a thrift store that were perfect, and as luck would have it, the store had a case of them. Marnie took it as her personal mission to come up with the right flowers for the vases. They had to be just the right color combination. She liked purple and yellow wildflowers the best and created a low profile arrangement so the flowers would not block conversation at the tables. One evening, Marnie bounced into Monica's room with a finished blue vase. She handed it to Monica with pride. When Monica complimented Marnie on how beautiful the arrangement was, Marnie said, "I wanted the vases to be stable so I put weight on the bottom by adding some marbles!"

It was an instant epiphany. "Marbles," Monica said out loud. She thought of Conor and his green cat's-eye marble. She did not even consult Joyce. She knew that there could be no better name for her shop than "Marbles." Monica decided to place a large glass bowl filled with marbles by the cash register. She thought it would be nice to give a marble to a customer every now and then.

Both Joyce and Monica were in agreement that Marbles would be a place where they could share a message of hope with others. This made their joint venture bigger than a business. It was a way for each of them to fulfil a purpose.

Joyce's gregarious personality made her the obvious choice to handle marketing and public relations for Marbles. It was her idea to create a "Family & Friends" reception for the neighborhood on Friday night and a public grand opening for the entire week after. Boxes of cinnamon rolls with invitations were sent to both Monica's and Joyce's previous workplaces and current churches and to Joyce's Rotary Club. Joyce also placed ads in the local papers and sent cinnamon rolls to some morning radio hosts in Chicago.

Monica saw CiCi again on the train several months after their first meeting. They happily exchanged addresses and telephone numbers. When Monica called to tell her about the opening of Marbles, CiCi was thrilled. Monica hoped she would see Conor and his mom at the grocery store again, but the red-haired boy with the string of freckles across his nose never seemed be at the store when Monica was shopping. She had hoped that Conor would get to experience the celebration of her journey that began with a little boy, a bag of marbles, and a pure expression of gratitude.

Monica realized that even though the grand opening celebration was a necessary step, just like the other steps she had taken, there would never be a final step on her personal journey. The principles would need to be repeated to help her continue to grow and evolve. But a gratitude marble would always symbolize her starting point, and now Marbles reminded her of the last principle in the circular process: giving back.

Often when Monica experienced moments of doubt and fear, her touchstone was the green marble. Each time she held it in her hand, she managed to reconnect with gratitude. It was easy to get caught up in all the unknowns of starting a business. "Would there be enough customers?" "Could she compete against the big coffee chains?" "Would she be able to support Marnie and Josh through college without going bankrupt?" These uncertainties would feed her fear if she let them. But the daily process of listing all the things for which she was thankful and regularly reviewing her seven words helped refocus her energy back to her purpose.

Monica exercised choice everyday to find daily joy. She made sure to experience the beauty of fresh-cut flowers, take regular walks outside, and enjoy inspirational literature. All of these things helped her connect with daily joy, and when she felt daily joy, she found that she attracted more joy into her life. Even Joyce could tell when Monica let this habit momentarily slip. She would gently remind Monica to "go out and find some joy" when she sensed that Monica needed it.

Monica developed a habit of reviewing her vision board every year to define new desires. Through working at her store, she made new friends or connected with current friends nearly everyday. This gave her the positive support she needed and provided many opportunities to give back. One day, Monica concluded that, indeed, her life had become abundant.

The reception and grand opening went smoothly. Earl and Joyce worked the room like a true host and hostess. Joyce was her typical gregarious self, and Earl charmed everyone. He truly believed that the cinnamon rolls at Marbles were the best in the world and was not afraid to share his opinion with anyone.

During the friends and family reception, Monica was amused when she caught Marty visiting with the young woman with colorful braids and clothing from the park. She smiled to herself as she realized that they both seemed to be enjoying the conversation! Stefan and Jenna couldn't have been more pleased with the décor and vision of Marbles. They paid her the highest compliment when they confidentially told Monica that Stefan's grandfather would have been right at home in Marbles. CiCi sent her regrets that she would be unable to attend the reception. But she stopped by on Wednesday during the first week of business, and she looked classic in her pink suit.

Monica had even invited the banker who helped her secure a small business loan to open Marbles. He seemed like an authentic person who really cared about her business and vision. His compassion touched Monica so she had shared a little more of her story with him. While Monica did not feel ready for a serious relationship, she was feeling comfortable about the idea of developing more male friendships. She decided that openness to a relationship was a natural progression in her journey, and she was surprised at how pleased she felt when he actually came to the reception.

About ten months after she had opened Marbles, on a warm summer morning, Monica received the best surprise of all. When she heard the tranquil door chime announcing a customer, she looked up from filling containers of cream and prepared to bid a Marbles welcome. When she saw who the customers were, Monica opened her mouth but nothing came out. A red-haired boy had entered Marbles with his mother. He was taller, and his hair was shorter, but Monica recognized him instantly. Conor had come to Marbles! She knew that they would not remember her, but she remembered them.

His mother ordered a hot tea, telling the girl behind the counter that she had heard such great things about Marbles. Monica stepped up to the counter and smiled at Conor then at his mother. Looking at Conor, she said, "I bet you like cinnamon rolls—don't you?" Conor grinned and nodded. "Would you like one?" Conor nodded again and looked with hope in his eyes to his mother. Before either one of them could say a word, Monica said to the girl behind the counter, "Please get this young man the biggest cinnamon roll you can find, my compliments." Monica reached into the glass bowl and picked out two green cat's-eye marbles. "Here," she said, handing one to Conor and one to his mother. "A little boy once taught me an important lesson with this simple marble. Carry it with you and remember to be grateful for the good things you already have in your life." Monica smiled at both of them as her employee handed Conor his cinnamon roll. This time, without prompting from his mother, Conor said, "Thank you." And it was a beautiful thing.

 Monica had returned with a warm cinnamon roll and three forks. She sat next to Edith and gave Joyce a look that said, "I'll take it from here." "Edith, my story continues to evolve everyday, but I escaped the joyless zone by living these principles. Your story is just beginning, and I think you are so fortunate. You get to have so many wonderful and exciting experiences on your personal journey. I hope you continue to visit Marbles and share your story with us."

Edith looked hopefully at Monica then Joyce. Her eyes seemed to say, "Do you really think I can do this?" Monica stood and held up her hand to say, "I'll be right back." She strolled over to the counter and reached into the bowl of marbles. She returned to the table and sat down. Looking into Edith's eyes, Monica took Edith's hand and smiled. Monica placed a few marbles into Edith's hand then gently closed Edith's fingers around them.

Monica said, "These marbles are like seeds of gratitude that you can plant anytime you wish. Your heart will prompt you when to use them." Edith looked at Joyce as if waiting for further instruction. Joyce smiled tenderly and said, "You will know when to give them away, Edith. Just let your intuition guide you. You can do it."

"Remember to:
1. Be Grateful.
2. Find Daily Joy.
3. Turn Down the Noise.
4. Imagine Your Dreams.
5. Connect with Support.
6. Do Something You Have Never Done.

"When you apply these principles, there will come a time that you will be ready to experience the last step, the one that feels the best because it creates its own energy. This step will keep you from ever returning to the joyless zone, Edith. This last step is 'give back.'"

Edith took a deep breath and looked at the marbles in her hand. It had been easy to listen to Monica and Joyce's story. The story made sense and gave her hope. She was sitting in a shop that was created by following these principles, and she had personally experienced the fruits of being grateful and finding daily joy. She felt more confident than she did on her first visit to Marbles. Monica and Joyce had told her that they believed in her and that her personal journey would be a never-ending process. They believed enough in her to ask her to begin sharing the principles with others. This assignment felt affirming *and* scary. But, what did she have to lose by trying? At that moment, Edith decided the principles would work for her, too, and she made an emotional commitment to leave the JZ forever.

Edith finished her last sip of hot chocolate, stood to leave, and began walking towards the door of Marbles. She stopped and turned back once more to smile at Monica and Joyce, to scan the vision boards, and to gather her courage. As she exited Marbles that Saturday afternoon, the tranquil door tone once again chimed, this time to announce that another customer had found her marbles.

About the Authors

Clare Sente, MS, RD

I have enjoyed twenty years as a health educator, speaker and wellness consultant. Growing up in a family that encouraged healthy eating and physical activity, it felt natural to study nutrition and teach others how to eat better. My world changed when my oldest sister was killed in a car accident my senior year in college. I was in graduate school during my grieving process and discovered that even though I continued to eat well and exercise, I often felt bad and would get sick. This experience expanded my focus on health to include the mind, body, and spirit.

The seven principles we outline in our book, originated after my participation in a health coach training program where I learned to slow down and practice mindfulness. I escaped my own "joyless zone" in the years after my divorce and left behind a pattern that included minimizing my talents and doubting my decisions. Discovering and listening to my intuition has been my greatest gift and has led to my biggest adventures yet, including writing this book, creating financial stability, visiting Africa, Spain, and New Zealand, starting my own business, speaking my truth, and imagining my soul mate, Todd, into my life.

After attending the Winter Wellness Forum in 2006, I set the intention of writing a book in a story format to teach these seven principles. A mentor advised, "If you can accomplish a goal on your own, the goal may not be big enough." I asked Troy to write this book with me and together we created a story neither of us could have written alone. If you would like more information about my workshops, teleseminars, or keynotes, please go to www.clarityliving.com.

TROY B. ADAMS, PHD

When I was in the 4th grade, I shoved a classmate. On my way to see the principal, my teacher intercepted me. She asked why I would do such a thing. I said that I didn't know and that I was very sorry.

With her arms folded, she looked at me with love in her eyes and quietly said that she expected more from me. At that moment, she happened to find a marble lying in the grass. She handed it to me and said it would remind me to be kind to others. I still have that marble. Her act of kindness inspired an important part of this story.

This teacher also told me that I had the gift of writing. Since the 4th grade, I have written poetry, short stories, and other creative works. Later in life, I wrote a dissertation, scientific articles and grants. To help me reconnect with the power of creative writing after a long academic career, I now keep a monthly wellness blog at wellnessmoment.com.

In all my years of writing, I can honestly say that rarely has the writing process been as inspirational and fun as it was during the creation of this book. Clare and I have come to know and love the characters in this story and we know you will too.

On a professional note, I consider myself a recovering academic. I co-founded a wellness company (wellsteps.com). I created and host an annual retreat in Sedona, Arizona where my friends and I help people identify and realize their intentions (winterwellnessforum.com). I have been told that my Louis Armstrong impersonation is pretty good! To contact me for a speaking engagement or to hear me sing, email me at drtroy@cox.net.